For Jamie, who loves swans.

With thanks to Rosemary Miner, President of the Western New York Pheasant and Waterfowl Association and to Joe Johnson, Chief Wildlife Biologist at the W. K. Kellogg Bird Sanctuary of Michigan State University for so generously sharing their expertise and to Renee' Cho, my agent, to Dorothy Goeller, my editor, to Diane Kianka, to Mimi Glass and to my fellow workshoppers, who diligently read my manuscripts.

W.P.

 Published by Silver Press
A Division of Simon & Schuster
299 Jefferson Road, Parsippany, NJ 07054

Designed by Brooks Design

Printed in the United States of America

ISBN 0-382-39325-2 (LSB) 10 9 8 7 6 5 4 3 2 1
ISBN 0-382-39324-4 (PBK) 10 9 8 7 6 5 4 3 2 1

Library of Congress Cataloging-in-Publication Data

Pfeffer, Wendy
Mute swans/by Wendy Pfeffer.
p. cm.—(Creatures in White)
Summary: Discusses the characteristics and life cycle of the Mute Swan.
1. Mute swan—Juvenile literature. [1. Mute swan. 2. Swans.] I. Title. II. Series: Pfeffer, Wendy. Creatures in White.
QL696.A52P45 1996 95-52709
598.4'1-dc 20 CIP AC

Photo credits: Photo research: Susan Van Etten; Cover, ©Peter Weimann /Animals, Animals; Back Cover, Manfred Danegger/©Tony Stone Images; 3, ©Manfred Danegger/Peter Arnold, Inc.; 4-5, ©Peter Weimann /Animals, Animals; 6-7, ©John Colwell/Grant Heilman, Inc.; 8-9 ©Peter Weimann /Animals, Animals; 10-11,©Manfred Danegger/Peter Arnold, Inc.; 12-13, ©Roland Seltre/Peter Arnold, Inc.; 14-15, ©George H. Harrison/Grant Heilman, Inc.; 16-17, ©Guenter Ziesler/Peter Arnold, Inc.; 18-19, ©Grant Heilman/Grant Heilman, Inc.; 20-21, ©Manfred Danegger/Peter Arnold, Inc.; 22-23, ©Michael De Young/Alaska Stock Images; 24-25, ©Lon E. Lauber/Alaska Stock Images; 26-27, ©Ake Lindau/Okapia 1989/Photo Researchers, Inc.; 28-29, ©Robert Maier/Animals, Animals; 30, ©Teioi Saga 1979/PPS/Photo Researchers, Inc.; 30, ©1986 J. Cancalos/Stock Boston; 30, ©B. Badsby/Academy of Natural Sciences/Vireo; 31, ©Tim Davis/Photo Researchers, Inc.; 31, ©Susan Van Etten; 31, ©Larry Cameron, 1985/Photo Researchers, Inc.; 31, ©Jeff Lepore 1990/Photo Researchers, Inc.; End Paper, ©Larry Lefever/Grant Heilman, Inc.

CREATURES IN WHITE

MUTE SWANS

by Wendy Pfeffer

Silver Press

Parsippany, New Jersey

A bright morning sun warms the water in Swan Lake. Over the trees surrounding the lake, large snowy white birds circle. Heading down, they stretch their wings and spread their webbed feet outward as if to put on the brakes. Tipping from side-to-side, they glide onto the water. Ripples spread out in circles as each majestic white bird touches down.

Spring has arrived at Swan Lake. And so have the swans. Year after year, the same pair of mute swans returns. They build a nest, raise their young, and stay until the weather cools.

Clouds, driven by the wind, move swiftly across the sky. The swans raise their wings up high and use them as white sails while the wind pushes them across the water.

In a sheltered spot each swan dips its long curved neck down in the water, searching for insects, seeds, and water plants to eat. The female needs more food than the male, since her body will soon produce eggs.

To get ready for egg-laying, the male, called a cob, and the female, called a pen, build a nest. The cob stands near their chosen site. He fills his bill with sticks, sedge, moss, and pondweed, then tosses them over his shoulder into a pile. The pen arranges the nesting mound with her bill, her breast, and her feet. She forms a shallow cup in the center and lines it with soft grasses.

Suddenly, the cob hisses a warning. Another swan has strayed near the pair's nest. The cob struts around his territory. He raises his wing feathers, ruffles his neck feathers, and lays his head back, hissing louder and louder. Then he rushes in the water with a great lashing of wings until the other swan retreats.

For the next ten days, the cob guards the nest while the pen lays six large greenish eggs. Then she sits on the eggs, and plucks fluffy white down from her breast to line the nest.

When she leaves to find food, she covers her eggs with the white fluff to keep them warm. The fluff also hides the eggs from enemies, like crows or ravens, who want to snatch and devour them.

In a nearby field the pen finds grain to eat. She raises and jerks her head, shaking the food down her gullet. Satisfied, she hurries back to the eggs.

The pen turns each egg often with her bill to make sure all the eggs are warmed evenly. By accident, one of them rolls out from under her. She stands up, sticks out her neck, and hooks her lower bill over the egg to roll it back into the nest.

After about thirty-two days, the baby swan inside one egg begins to breathe and makes a faint clicking sound. Inside another egg a tiny unhatched swan cheeps. The mother answers by calling softly. The cob stands guard, ready to attack foxes, dogs, people, or any other threat to the eggs.

About thirty-three days after the pen began to sit on the eggs, they begin to hatch. The baby uses its egg tooth, sharp as a thorn, to break through the shell. Thin cracks form near the tiny hole.

The baby bird rests for a while. Then it turns around inside the shell, pecking a circle of holes as it turns. The baby rests, then pecks some more. After almost two whole days of hard work, a tired, wet, gray baby swan enters a big new world. Five more eggs crack open, and five more tired, wet, gray baby swans appear.

The babies, called cygnets, can wobble and walk soon after they hatch. They're covered with down. In a few hours the cygnets' down dries and fluffs up.

With the pen and cob guiding, the family goes for its first swim. The cygnets' necks are too short to reach down into the water for food. The parents paddle their feet to stir up insects. With the tasty bugs at the surface, the hungry cygnets gobble them down.

During the day the swan family swims among the lily pads while grasshoppers sing. Crickets chirp at night, and warm spring days become hot summer days.

The family paddles around, scooping worms and plants off the water. Each bird places its lower bill along the top of the water. It draws water and food in at the front of its bill. Then it squirts the water out sideways. Wiggly bugs trapped inside a swan's mouth make a very tasty meal.

Suddenly, a mink appears. It slips into the water and swims toward the cygnets. The cob hisses, raises his wings, and lifts out of the water ready to attack. The cygnets sense the danger. Each one opens its mouth, raises its tongue, and lunges forward. The pen joins in with a great beating of wings. Hissing loudly, the whole family surges forward, and the mink disappears under the water. The danger is over, for now.

For a while the cygnets stay close to their parents. They climb onto the cob's back, scrambling between his white wings and tail. He helps by making a "step" with his foot. Once on top, the cygnets snuggle under the cob's wings, so only their heads are seen. The six "cheep, cheep, cheep" as they are taxied around Swan Lake.

By late summer the downy fluff covering the cygnets is replaced by white feathers. The pen and cob show the cygnets how to take off and land. The young birds stay aloft for a few moments. Then they splash into the lake. With much wing flapping and water splashing, the cygnets learn to fly.

When fall comes to Swan Lake, sugar maples turn yellow, and swamp maples turn a fiery red. Flocks of white trumpeter swans fly overhead. Their loud trumpetlike calls echo in the air as they migrate to warmer waters.

The days grow shorter and the nights cooler. Frogs, turtles, and water snakes bury themselves under the mud at the bottom of the lake to hibernate. Bugs, plants, and other food for the swans become scarce. Soon ice will cover Swan Lake like a blanket. It's time for the swan family to migrate.

On a moonlit night, when the wind is right, the family lifts off with a white dazzle of feathers and a great flapping of wings. As they fly, their wings make a soft whooshing sound. On their way south the swans keep in touch with each other by listening for the rhythm of the "whoosh, whoosh, whoosh."

They join other groups of white swans and fly in V-shaped wedges. The flock follows familiar rivers and mountains. They use the sun, moon, and stars to guide them, too.

In clear weather they fly high and fast. When the weather is bad, they fly close to the ground. Flocks stop for food and rest along the way.

The pen and cob stay at the same wintering grounds every year. There the family swims and eats together. The parents still protect and teach their young.

Days grow longer. The weather warms. The swan family migrates north to Swan Lake. The parents will raise a new brood. The young will stay with them for about four years. Then they will go off to another lake, pond, or dammed-up stream. Each will find a mate, build a nest, and raise its young.

A bright morning sun warms the water in Swan Lake. The ice has melted. Buds on the maple trees swell. Sometimes spring arrives early at Swan Lake, and sometimes late. But it always comes.

And so do the swans.

Swan Facts

black swan

- Mute swans are not really mute, or silent. They make barking sounds to call their young and hissing sounds to chase enemies.

- It takes ten days for the pen to lay six eggs. She does not sit on them until the last egg is laid so all of the eggs will hatch at the same time.

- Often in cold climates, swans have been known to bring a stone into their nests to help keep their eggs warm when the pen leaves the nest to eat.

- With a tailwind, a flock of swans might fly fifty to sixty miles an hour. With a strong headwind, they may only reach a speed of twenty or thirty miles an hour.

whooper swan

trumpeter swan

Coscoroba swan

tundra swan

■ Each spring mute swans, who mate for life, return to the same nesting sites.

■ When flying in the V formation, the swan in front gets most of the wind. It's tiring. After a while, another swan takes the lead.

■ There are two kinds of mute swans in the world. English mute swans have gray cygnets. Eurasian mute swans have white cygnets.

■ There are at least seven other species of swans in the world: trumpeter, tundra, whooper, and Bewick's swans live north of the equator. The black, black-necked, and Coscoroba swans live south of the equator.

Bewick's swan

black-necked swan